AWENYDD

by

Blodwen E Jones

Grosvenor House
Publishing Limited

This book is published by
Grosvenor House Publishing Ltd
Link House
140 The Broadway, Tolworth, Surrey, KT6 7HT.
www.grosvenorhousepublishing.co.uk

A CIP record for this book
is available from the British Library

ISBN 978-1-83975-906-2

Warning: contains explicit language of a sexual nature

This book is for ALL the amazing NHS staff I've met during the latest part of my journey. Then it's for the 3 lovely ladies, who were with me in the Covid-free bay, on Northumberland ward, St Thomas' Hospital.

They will never know just how much they helped me to truly realise and accept myself! Finally, many thanks to all my long suffering family, friends and yes - even acquaintances, who have put up with my foibles etc. That includes the help I've had getting my books together - something I can hardly believe at times!

Blessings and thanks to each and every one of you.

BIO

This is Blod's second book of poems, and it's looking like there could be a third! Her creative juices are flowing freely!

Here, she shares some old poems she found doing a deep clean during the first lock down. The rest have been written since her first book "MOONSTRUCK" was published.

She apologises for the shortage of humour within these pages, but 2020 was NOT a fun filled year for so many people.

She is ever hopeful that she will continue to find a way through the difficult life path she's been travelling.

She intends to have as much fun as possible anyway, and why not?

PROEM

Getting my first book "MOONSTRUCK" published was an epic journey!
It was fraught with difficulties, but the synchronicities kept me going.
From meeting Jenessa Qua on a hot Saturday in June 2019, to my book going on sale last year on the 31st of March 2020, was like giving birth!
9 months it took, and a lot of the poems were written towards the end of 2019, and with hindsight.

My planned launch didn't happen because of the pandemic! (Perhaps it will be a double launch at the end of this year - 2020 - who knows?)

I took the opportunity to self isolate, and started dealing with the mess my home is/was in.
As a woman with various health challenges, it was a case of - "slowly, slowly, catchee monkey."
I sort of started in my bedroom, where I discovered some buried treasure - or was it?
Going through a box of what had been ignored for MANY years, I discovered some poems. They were from the 70's to the 80's, 1 with no date, and 1 from '98!
I hadn't realised I still had them, or even that I'd written them. It's definitely my handwriting, although a helluva lot smaller making it difficult to read them. Having said that though, I did recall writing them as I read them!

As I started working through them, typing them up on the tablet (2nd hand) I'd bought toward the end of 2019, I couldn't believe some of the drivel I'd written!
The first however many, were written after my relationship with my 2nd husband ended.
Considering the fact that there was a heck of a lot wrong with the relationship, makes my writing total twaddle!

I fairly quickly decided that the title for the chapter containing them would be called "LOVES YOUNG **BLOODY** DREAM!"

There are the odd ones that don't really fit into that category, but I wanted to keep them all in order of how I'd written them.

Don't ask me why, as I don't have a clue!

I am/was also writing poems for this book and processing BIG TIME!

Being stuck in a first floor flat with NO balcony and the sun pouring through my EXTREMELY dirty windows, I was reminded of my school days.

I recall looking out of the window and wishing I was out there in the sunshine.

I am NOT the sunbathing type, but I do enjoy the warmth of Grandather Sun's rays and the way he illuminates our home, Mother Earth.

During this time of Sacred Sanctuary (lock down) as I have heard it called, I was watching something on YouTube and they said we need to be asking ourselves the question - "why am I here?"

My immediate flippant thought was - "because I'm in bloody lock down!" I knew exactly what he meant though.

My 67th birthday earlier this month of April 2020, passed in a blur of responding to texts, emails and phone calls about a variety of things, including birthday greetings.

I felt truly blessed for having the means to maintain contact in ways that have become available in fairly recent times.

This set me thinking about how technology has advanced since the calculator came out around 1963.

We weren't allowed to use them, as they were considered as cheating. We had to use a book called a Ready Reckoner.

Hard to believe that nowadays computers are necessary for doing school work etc!

My first landline was installed in 1980 after coming to live in London, when my daughter was taken ill, and I didn't have the means to call a doctor etc at the time.

In 1982, the guy I was living with and I, bought the kids a ZX SPECTRUM for Christmas as a joint present.
It didn't take long for it to be commandeered by my son!

I was given my first mobile in the late 90's, and all it could do was make and receive calls and texts. It was very similar to the hand held communicators in the original series of Star Trek! Now my mobile does everything but the dishes!

My first laptop is still around, but I haven't used it for a looong time. I have been trying to remember when I bought it. It was after 2008. (I have managed to find a good home for it now.) As for my notebook which replaced it, it is thinner, lighter and around the same size.

Now my tablet is flavour of the moment!

Thinking about all of this, it's struck me how much simpler life was in the 70's, for me at any rate.
Perhaps what is happening now will lead to a life that is not so fast paced and more caring.
Somewhere along the way, our sense of community has become fragmented and non-existent in a lot of areas.
People walk along with their eyes glued to their devices and their ears covered with the latest set of headphones!
It saddens me to see very young children in their prams holding a device, and being bombarded with what sounds to me like unadulterated rubbish.
I have seen mothers on their phones, ignoring the desperate pleas of their child to be given some attention.
I make a point of telling women how glad I am to see them without a phone and interacting with their child.

I feel the need to mention, that I was coming to terms with the realisation that I don't have to worry about finding a job now, and then the pandemic struck! Ok! I know. I'd been retired for nearly 2 years!

My retirement age was upped by 5 years, as I was a few days the wrong side of the retire at 60 brigade for women!
I really felt that the retirement age for men, should have been reduced to 60. This would have given younger people the opportunity to work etc.
I recently heard that there is talk of reducing the retirement age to 50!
I don't know if it is true, but I think it's a very good idea.

It's now mid-February 2021, and a lot of shit has gone down the pan and into the sewer, literally and metaphorically speaking!

Mr Tibbs passed on to the Happy Hunting Grounds on December 18th last year.
I would be lying if I said that I don't miss him, but it truly was a blessing in disguise.
I was finding it more difficult to clean up after him, because bending was very uncomfortable.
His health had never been good, and he deteriorated fast.

I was in the process of having a lot of tests to find out what was causing the pain in my spleen and abdomen.
Turned out I had a cancerous tumour in the upper right side of my bowel!
It was removed on the 28th of January by the lovely surgeon Mr George.
I will be eternally grateful to him and all the lovely people who have been involved in getting me sorted.

The journey isn't over yet, but I am optimistic and I have plans in the making.
I truly hope that you will find something to inspire you within these pages.
Remember that life is a journey full of lessons you can choose to ignore or embrace.
I wish you love, light and healing on your journey.

CHAPTER 1

LOVES YOUNG **BLOODY** DREAM

1976?

Since that first night - so long ago,
when I looked up and saw you there,
our love has strengthened and deepened too,
and now our lives we live and share.

At times we may have ups and downs,
but all along the joy is felt,
of living and loving - our lives as one -
you and me - the whole - complete.

So my love - my heart's desire,
whatever pitfalls life may hold,
we two together will face the world,
our love a shield to make us bold.

JULY OR AUGUST 1977 - HOSPITAL

When first I fell in love with you -
the Earth was green - the heavens blue.
The stars shone down on our new love -
no clouds to mar the sky above.
The gods looked down and blessed our life -
and we were joined as man and wife.
But soon dark clouds were to appear -
as I reached out to you my dear.
Your heart grew colder day by day -
then finally you turned away.
The weather's changed, my arms grow cold -
I have no lover left to hold.
My heart is broken, torn in two,
for 'though you hate, I still love you.

EARLY AUGUST 1977

Each day was filled with thought of you
the dream I'd had - at last come true.
From here on in, calm paths to walk -
to love and live, to fight to talk.
My life had reached a different turning,
no more the want, the need, the yearning.
In you I'd found the ideal one -
the Earth, the moon, the sky and sun.
I gave my all, my every part,
my love, my life, my very heart.
YOU were my world, my whole existence,

all barriers down and little resistance.
But in all my loving I could not see -
that you had no real need of me.
You took it all within your stride -
not caring - with your arrogance and pride.
But one day you will realise -
that only hurt can come from lies.
When you in need to someone turn -
they'll walk away, and you will learn.

EARLY AUGUST 1977

Life isn't just a game to play,
but each moment you feel the pull.
And now to living from day to day -
enjoy it, live it to the full.
Take each chance you have to live -
reach out and touch, feel the thrill -
take all there is, and all to give -
make that new start, although uphill.
When love's been lost -
and dreams are shattered
no matter that your heart the cost,
nor you the one who really mattered.
Forget the past and start anew -
a life so different from the last.
Now live it, and think of the two -
who are your future, present and past.

EARLY SEPTEMBER 1977

The mist has cleared,
the mirage is dispersed.
I see him as he really was -
an illusion created just for me.
And now I face reality -
the man I love is dead to me -
and never more will he return.

23rd SEPTEMBER 1977

I had to hide my inner turmoil -
the churning and turbulence deep in me.
We talked of mundane matters -
but my heart was crying out to you.
When at last we were on the right track -
you refused to take the turning back
and I laid my soul at your feet.
Circles, 'round and 'round it went, 'til -
at last I felt that talk was done -
and you would go - into your other life.
In my acceptance of the end I found -
that where there's love and life, there's hope and a chance.
Through the mist of my eyes I felt I saw -
some flicker of the man I love,
past is past, what's done is done.
If there's a future, then let it be.
Oh! God, look down on us and draw us closer still -

for my life alone is no joy to me.
I need to hold the man I love -
to share our joys and troubles -
forever, together - into eternity.

22nd OCTOBER

Help me forget the love I've lost -
my heart is tortured, I've paid the cost.
Oh! God above - look down on me -
see my pain - set me free.
How to erase the pain, the sorrow -
forget the past and face tomorrow?
I can't go on in misery -
knowing my loved one - loves not me.
I can't accept that it's all ended -
will this heart of mine 'er be mended?
If only - but that's an age old phrase -
I could awake from this mad haze.
To accept would be pure heaven -
but up to now - I can't, not even
though I know he does not care -
it doesn't ease the hurt I bear.
My love for him is deeply set -
since that first night we really met.
How to erase the pain and sorrow -
forget the past then face tomorrow?
How indeed? I wish I knew -
for if I did, I could forget you.

30th OCTOBER 1977

Is my love for the man I lived with -
or is it for the man I married?
Are they one and the same - am
I right in thinking that they're not?
How do I tell the two apart -
when the first one captured my heart?
Will the man I love return to me -
and things be as they used to be?
I don't suppose I'll ever know.
For ages now he hasn't shown,
so I must go on from day to day -
feeling my way through the mists of time.
Perhaps one day, the sun will shine again -
I only hope it doesn't take too long.

MARCH 1978

When loves young dream has come and gone,
and sweet memories still linger on,
when to forget would be sweet release,
no hurt, ache, yearning, just peace.

If all this could be, I'd be content -
but in this life, for me it's not meant.
Must all my days be an agony -
is there not something better for me?

But the gods my path have drawn,
must I travel along - alone - forlorn?
Perhaps one day I'll find out why -
my heart must ache, my eyes must cry

31st MARCH 1978

What is this feeling left in me -
is it loneliness, hurt or misery?
Each of these and more I feel -
has it happened, is it real?
More days have come, and more have gone -
and yet it stays, it lingers on.
A word, a phrase, a place, a time -
can bring that pain - so sublime.
I always think, I always feel -
is it true, can it be real?
Will I awake from deep slumber -
and these sad days have had no number?
Or will we stay our separate ways?
God knows, I don't want this haze.
I want what's right and meant to be -
us two united - you and me.
Will it ever come to pass -
have I the right to even ask?
Can I for once have what's my right -
without this constant - endless fight?

My life may not have been well lived -
but for two whole years I know I did.
I lived, I loved, I cared, I shared and gave -
I wanted it to continue beyond the grave.
If there's a god, then hear my prayer -
and unite us again - our lives to share.

31st MARCH 1978

As you awoke from your slumber -
you looked so innocent and angelic.
I took you in my arms and carried you.
I took you to your land of dreams -
to a place I cannot reach you.
A place of peace, of fantasy and light -
so small, so beautiful, and yet so -
I cannot find the words to tell you.
The ones I use are most unfair -
but in reality, I love - I care.
My heart aches and hurts for the way I am -
I love so deeply the two of you -
but it's not easy - the things you do.
I try so hard, but don't succeed.
The needs you have I can't fulfil -
because of circumstances - not of me.
If the world were mine - I'd give it to you.
But my angels, dream your dreams -
I'll try my best to fulfill your schemes.
Sleep well, and God watch over you.
I love you both, and always will.

5th APRIL 1978

The time we have in life is short.
What is one lifetime in so much?
And in that space we have to live
we are nothing, no-one, insignificant.
But if we have a purpose to fulfill
dream, a promise, our life to share.
Then though so precious be that time
we have used and spent it well.
Think on these things, my own true love,
for tomorrow may never be.
The only thing for sure - is here and now,
is there a now where you want to stay?
Could you face your possible tomorrows
knowing you have lost what means most?
Or is it in your heart to share your time?
I wish that space could be for me.
You made a promise - have you forgot?
Eternity - you said - it may not be far off.

a

5th APRIL 1978

One day I met a lovely man
little did I know he had a plan.
He got me into my own bed
from then on in, I was led.
He fooled me for nigh on two years,
and left me shocked and in tears,
after two months of wedded bliss,

and not so much that went amiss.
He'd gone away to work you see,
so I didn't see to much of he.
I didn't see too much of t'other
he might as well 'ave been my brother.
You've heard of housewives excuses
well he's the one who used those ruses.
I thought what's up here what's the score
not much of him and that's for sure.
And now alas I'm a celibate
that gives no cause to cheer at any rate.
But to have him back is what I need
not 'cos I'm feeling sexual greed.
Because although he's a rotten basket
I love him still, need you ask it.

25th APRIL 1978

What of this nightmare that was not so.
Although so real, it seems a dream.
Can it be, it really happened?
The knowledge is there, it's his in three.
I feel so numbed that this could be,
and yet it was, we know we three.
What of tomorrow and forever more?
What is our existence really for?
The apple cart of life is ever upset.
For I at least, it does seem so.
I know not whence I've been or go.

25th APRIL 1978

E'en so I dwell in a whirlpool of living.
Forever spinning and drawing me down.
There are two sweet things that pull me back
they have no reason to save my existence.
Except that of the umbilical cord
A cord so pure and ne'r true cut
a chain that binds us into one.
Each, individual, yet United,
by love, by hate, right and family.
I don't deserve their love and purity.
But if not for them, I would not be.
In all this insanity, which is mine alone
they keep me safe, and anchor me in my storm.
Will they ever know their true worth to me
for I am not the best, that theirs should be.
They deserve a patient, understanding mother.
But poor sweet angels, they've me instead.
I try so hard, but don't succeed.
To help, to cherish, to share our needs.
For the one, and three we are.
We need, we have, we love each other
I hope and pray, this will be enough.

2nd JULY 1978

And so the wheel of time grinds on.
I feel less the hurt and much more sane.
The memories shine on, as the sun

I can't forget the loving pain.
But now I find the going easier
as the past I try to push away.
My days are lighter and much breezier
and on this path I hope to stay.
Although my life seems dull and dreary,
and time oft' hangs heavy on my hands,
at times I feel so unutterably weary.
I think of future different lands.
Lands so full of milk and honey,
of love and laughter, gaiety and joy
of times when we won't be so lonely
the future with my girl, my boy.
There is no denying of Kismet our fate
and I believe it will come full tide
when it does, it will be worth the wait.
'Til then on the wheel of time, we'll ride.

11th JULY 1978

What star is shining on this life of mine
that I should be so unlucky allowed the time.
Why is it that life is so complicated.
Each moment of joy so soon outdated.
Why must I go on doing the giving
while others take and go on living.
Is there an answer to this rhyme
Perhaps I'll know - given time.

29th AUGUST 1978 (AFTER OUR MEETING THE DAY BEFORE)

On the dawn of my re-awakening,
I little knew what fate held in store.
But then I sensed, and not mistaking,
when I saw you walk through the door.

On the eve of that great day
as we talked of this and that,
I looked into pools of blue, green, grey,
and then I knew where I was at.

In the night as we lay together,
I felt at last that I'd come home,
to the unity that goes on forever,
safe and loved, no more to roam.

As the second day was dawning,
I knew you'd have to go away.
Did you also feel that morning,
that you'd return to stay one day?

What has Kismet written down for me?
Will our futures follow the same line,
or separate to wander, each one free?
Or will our life threads intertwine?

12th SEPTEMBER 1978

Now I know what love's about.
It changes, turns you inside out.
The love that was no more can be,
the time is different, so is he.
The first love of youth is as a dream.
The second is not what it may seem.
The third an all devouring passion
a love that grows and doesn't lessen.
Something so deep, so pure, so true,
and in this loving, you can view
another time or place, a new tomorrow
with or without, a time to borrow
time from the one you have to share.
Does he know, does he really care?
If time there is, then time I'll take,
and in that time I hope to make
the man whose time is love to me
open his eyes and surely see
the love that was no more can be. The time is different, so is he.

2nd OCTOBER 1978 (A poem formed the day dad was buried the 25th Sept)

I see your face through a haze of tears,
I hear your voice through foggy time.
You reach out from another, distant place,
and touch my soul with your passing.
Our lives were joined in love and blood,

most moments shared along the way,
no more to talk, to hear with you.
For you've gone your way, and I go mine.
But until we meet in that far off place,
I'll cherish what we shared, and hope
against hope, that you understood,
that you knew I really cared.

APRIL 1979

Of life's illusions, love's the worst,
to fall in love it seems you're cursed.
Does love exist? Can it really be?
Has it happened in truth to me?
To have, to hold, to take away,
to wait and hope for another day.
A day of lasting love so true,
when the man you'll love - loves you.

28th APRIL 1979

Never more, never more, says the breeze.
All is lost, all is gone, say the trees.
Never more, never more says the rain,
all is lost, all is gone, except the pain.
Never more, never more, says my heart.
All is lost, all is gone, we had to part.

27th MAY 1986

When loves young dream has passed you by,
each passing phase was just a try.
One day you meet that real awakening -
and wait in dread for the bubbles breaking.
Your hearts and minds have met as one -
what's been before has long since gone.
You find that time takes on new meaning -
a moment, a day, a week or evening -
all meet, and upon a life - times knowing you -
of loving, living, sharing and growing.
Togetherness is what we share -
you know, and I know how much we care.
In days to come, we'll look back on this -
and nod our heads as we reminisce.

1st JUNE 1986

Deep in me
there's a feeling of -
liberation.
When I offered it to
the world -
it was sent back as
a multitude of poisonous
darts.
My new-found freedom -
and love of life,
was curtailed.

Because of convention -
and responsibility?
To turn my back on
flesh of my body,
cannot be done.
To walk away from truth -
and goodness, isn't in me.
So for now I have no choice -
but to walk a middle road.
Or -
lose my sanity.

14th MARCH 1987- WEDNESDAY 15th JULY 1998

You filled a void in my life.
I'd looked long, and hard
for someone who'd really care.
The love and laughter, even strife
have helped us to mark our card.
For the time we've had, and the time we'll share,
I love you, and I'll be there.

14th MARCH 1987

My heart cries out at the injustice of it all,
the years of buried prejudices.
The way home and society moulded me,
to become what they wanted to see.
When I found the truth and fought them,

I was labelled, radical, protester, liar.
Knowing the right, and they in their
narrow, bigoted, selves are wrong,
does not make it an easy task.
Seeing what they've done to those
they supposedly love, and feeling it,
makes me angry, confused and hurt.

14th MARCH 1987

I am woman.
My strength lies in the ability to
bounce back from all of life's problems.
I am woman.
Success lies in the curve of my breast,
the sway of my hips, the cave between my thighs.
I am woman.
My life was to marry, conceive, keep house,
nurse, be there, be dumb, be perfection.
I am me, and a woman.
There is life after finding yourself,
and it's better than you'd hoped for.

?

Is there a message in the music,
is it the beat of Mother Earths heart?
Do I have some task to fulfil

Preordained, past, present and future,
will prepare me for the role.
I feel expectant, waiting,
for the birth of -
I don't know what.

WEDNESDAY 15th JULY '98

You know I love you, so don't play fair.
Instead, you take a lion's share.
You thrive on attention, like the king of the beasts,
but never in famine, only in feasts.
When you've had enough, you snarl and roar
silently. Putting up barriers I refuse to ignore.
Does the king of the beasts run away,
or stay to conquer and rule for another day?

2nd JUNE 1986 - 14th MARCH 1987

They looked at me
and found me lacking,
set up court
and did their backing.
Them and us,
two against many.
How dare I commit this heinous crime,
you'll pay your dues - in time.
You'll not do this, you will do that,

who are they to say what's at?
We'll have your kids, we'll have your life,
here, be done, try a knife.
No matter what I do or say,
they mean to have their legal way.
My only crime in their blind eyes,
"To make a protest," no alibis.
"How can love come into this?"
are silent words of ignorance.
"What crime?" I hear you ask of me,
it's here, in black and white for all to see.

3rd JUNE 1986

The sound of your voice at the end of the line,
knowing you care, makes me feel fine.
The touch of your hand, the look in your eye,
make me feel special, ten feet high.

Things that you do, and the things you say,
make me feel wanted come the end of the day.
When you hold me in your arms at night,
I know that my world's just right.

Knowing you love me, and I love you,
nothing, and no-one else will do.

?

Sorrow
Loss
Fear
Release
Sadness
Worry
Hate
Unsure
Secure
Loved
Love
Lost
Found
Wanted
Needed
Cared for
Commitment

14th MARCH 1987

I want to write,
It's late at night.
I want to commit myself to paper.
I want to cry.
I need to try,

to put it all down on paper.
I'd like to scream,
I'd love to shout,
to show it to the world about.
Show them the truth,
show them I'm right.
How do I do it? It's late at night.

CHAPTER 2

THE ROCKY ROAD TO LOCKDOWN

PLANETARY VIBES!

I was out and about one day before lockdown was imposed on us,
I think it was late February, and I was off to catch a bus.
I was probably heading to the Maudsley for a meeting,
looking forward to catching up with friends and greeting
some with a HUG, as well as the usual 'hello'.
Will that ever happen again? Doesn't seem like it - no!
The point I'm really trying to get to is this,
there was something about the vibes that was totally amiss!
When I finally got home, I wrote down the idea
of a title for a poem, and it's finally become clear -
to me at any rate, you just might not agree.
It was a sense of what was coming, I now see!
I truly feel that we've been taken for a ride
through the current situation that's kept us inside.
We've been fed misinformation from day to day,
even the children weren't allowed out to play!
We were kept away from what made us happy and sane,
and I have a feeling it will happen again and again.

People have lost so much through this mad event,
and that includes lives that are totally spent.
Death has claimed many for one reason or another,
the virus, suicide, domestic violence and any other
things that may come to your mind.
The way we've been treated is very unkind.
How many people died all alone -
whether in hospital, or in their home?
What of the friends and family who couldn't honour the dead?
Need I say more, or has enough been said?
I really wish I had been given a genuine choice,
and the FACTS, so I could give voice
to why I wouldn't wear a mask, even if I was able.
I have COPD as it happens and my breathing isn't stable!
I haven't been anywhere, but to the local shops for supplies.
What has gone on there, has truly opened my eyes!
The current situation has brought out the worst in so many sheeple,
and fortunately, the best in very few people.
I don't have a clue where what's happening will end,
but I do have the feeling that THEY are setting a new trend!
I'm going to stop writing now, as I'm pissing myself off,
and have a swig of water as I'm ready to cough!

WEDNESDAY 18th MARCH 2020

This morning I got two letters in the post -
both offering life cover to people over fifty!
It made me consider how they're making the most
of the current situation and being pretty nifty
about sending out their blurb.

I think and feel it's all very underhand
doing this before the powers that be curb
us in all that we do. I can understand
the need for what's to come very soon.
Corona virus has taken the people by storm!
I feel it's going to get a lot of us to re-tune
our thinking. We're going to have to reform
the way we've been treating Mother Earth.
We all need to consider the whole picture,
especially now we've reached a dearth
of so much that was freely available. Stricture?
We 'ain't seen nothing yet!
What's going on now is going to get worse
before it can start to get better. You bet
there'll be times when we'll scream and curse -
we're only human when all's been said and done.
I wonder how the white rhino felt in his final days?
Did he realise all his kind were gone?
We need to stop being hellbent on the destruction
of the planet and really change our ways.

IN GRATITUDE

And it came to pass that many humans went to the "Happy Hunting Grounds".
This was as a result (to a certain extent) of their belief that IT'S not as bad as IT sounds!

They didn't follow the advice they'd been given.
Their need to stock up with pasta and loo roll was anxiety driven.

Obtaining some of the simplest things in life -
was difficult to say the least, causing endless strife.

People were fighting in the supermarket aisles -
over the most basic of things and there were very few smiles.

Life as we knew it, had definitely changed
and all we'd done before had to be rearranged.

Work, for some, was done from home - online.
For those with techno savvy, this was fine.

Some people cashed in on what was occurring,
while others went the extra mile preferring
to keep things like the food supply and the NHS going,
while the risks to their own health kept on growing.

There were those who went above and beyond the call of duty,
whose Souls shone with an exceptional beauty.
To each and every one of you, I give thanks -
for carrying on and not breaking ranks.

MEDICS OR POLICE?

Mr Tibbs was just sitting looking at me intently.
I was having a good moan and groan re the situation incidentally!
His puzzled look seemed to say -
"Who shall I call first, medics or police?
Perhaps I should get her to let me out,
clear off and head for Nice.
I hear there's a better class of feline females over there.
I wonder if they're all taken, or are any going spare?
She's gone quiet now, I'm off to have a break
and let her get on with her own stuff for goodness sake!

HUGS?

Why am I going down misery road?
Is it because I'm stuck in my abode -
for yet another 3 bloody weeks?
How many times does this virus have peaks?
8 weeks ago, I had plans for going out and about.
What's happening now's put our lives on hold, of that there's no doubt.
When I was heading into a psychosis one time, I wanted the world to stop, so I could get off!
Well now it's happened, and on the rare occasions I go out, as someone with
COPD I'm scared to cough!
I keep my social distance - 'cos I know I have to.
But those wearing face masks rarely do.
(Receiving and giving hugs, was something I had to learn,
'cos as a child we just never got them. It's true!)
Now I'm REALLY missing spending time with my friends.
Is this the way life's really going? I suppose it just depends -
on what's decided at the end of the day.
Do I really want to live my life like this? Absolutely not, no way.

OMFG!

I woke up this morning feeling like shit
and no matter how I tried, I couldn't get on with it.
It's a combination of so many things now
and I wish I really could show you how
I am struggling to get on with the day.
How do I find the words, what do I say?
"Oh my fucking god" is going through my head!
"Fuck it, I'm going back to my bed."

I just lay there with the thoughts churning.
All I wanted was to stop the yearning
for respite from the dreadful feeling
that made me aware of how much I was reeling
from the onslaught of daily life.
I wish I could cut through it all with a knife
like spreading some butter on bread.
All I'm getting is a feeling of dread.

I need something to ease my troubled mind.
Some gentle words from someone kind.
A none threatening hug from a good friend.
Support to keep me from this critical trend.
A way to shovel through all the shit
I'm dealing with and get on with it.
Tomorrow is another day
and I hope to feel in a good way.

BE NICE

What on Earth is she doing now for goodness sake?
I wish she'd clear off and give ME a much needed break -
from her huffing and puffing and talking out loud.
I'm really struggling to avoid going under a black cloud -
of wanting to tear up her net curtain again!
When she clocks what I've done she'll swear, shout and then
spend the rest of the day ignoring my pleas!
Be nice to me Blod. I'd love some of your cheese.

WHEN ALL'S SAID AND DONE

I am trying my level best, to avoid going into a deeper depression.
Hanging on to my already fragile marbles, has become a major obsession.
There's nowhere to go now, but a LOT I could do.
I feel like killing poor Tibby at times, but that's nothing new!
To be totally honest he's being worse than ever,
and wanting to send him back where he came from, isn't clever.
I've had him a long time now, and I really couldn't do that.
I have to remind myself, that when all's said and done - he is a cat.
They say pets are supposed to help to reduce your stress,
but all he seems to be good for, is pissing me off, and making a mess!
There is the odd occasion when he jumps on my lap
and treats me like a tree - sticking his sharp claws in - making me snap.
I really wish I could end this one in a positive way,
but the world is in crisis at the end of the day!
I know I'm not the only human going through a very tough time,
the thought of a fair and decent way of life, is truly sublime.

IT JUST WASN'T HAPPENING!

Suddenly it's time for bed, having been up since silly o'clock!
If my family and friends could see me now, I think they'd have a shock.
I guess I probably look very distracted, with my hair all over the place.
That would be 'cos I'm running my hands through it, to keep it off my face.
Anyway. My plants didn't get repotted, the job's been on my list for a while.
The bananas are still sitting in their skins, as I couldn't make the cake with a smile.
The dust is sitting on the shelves, and anywhere else it decided to settle.

The reason for my inactivity, is because I'm not in very good fettle!
Ok! So I have spoken to people on the phone, and I did do the dishes too.
I also prepared and cooked my dinner, that took quite a lot of time - it's true.
But as for being motivated to do something that's pleasure giving,
well, to be totally honest with you - it just wasn't happening!

JJ (Corona virus)

I was woken up at 5am today by the overpowering stench of Tibby's poo!
By 7am I was ready to kill him, as for the third time he wanted in - it's true!
He'd been demanding to be let out of the only door to the outside of my flat.
I'm on the first floor, so he can only go on the walkway and that is that!
But Mr Tibbs has other ideas for pissing me off every day -
he finds something new he can do that puts me in a mood that holds sway -
until I'm ready to go out and about. I am so glad having things to do and places to go,
and staying at home with him? I don't think so!

But now I really don't have any choice
I have to find a way to put up with his voice -
meowing to get his own way - now!
I really don't know how I'll manage him in the weeks ahead -
and thinking of listening to me - talking to myself - fills me with dread!
So far, the humour coming through has kept me going.
When there'll be an end to this, there is no knowing?
All I CAN do is keep soldiering on -
sending out loving and healing vibes for IT to be gone.

WEDNESDAY 22nd JULY

If I had a very powerful magic wand, I'd wave it to end this current nightmare.
I don't mean that would just be for me, people of the world too, would get their share.
I'm not quite sure how to set things right, I guess I'd offer it up to the UNIVERSE,
to correct things that have gone so horribly wrong. The way things are, it's as if a curse
has been placed on a large part of the human race! We don't know where the heck we are
when it all boils down to it. Truth is, THEY have us living in fear and I think it's a step to far.
THEY keep moving the goal posts on what we can and can't do.
Well let's be honest about this, THEY aren't following the laws they're passing! True???
Many years ago, when my head was in a whirl, I wanted the world to stop, so I could get off!
Now in an odd way it's happened, and every single person is REALLY afraid to cough!
It's a good way to get to the front of the queue in the shops that are serving us,
and to clear a large space around you, when you're finally allowed on a bus!
Having said that has just jogged my memory. Today I was filled with excitement
as I prepared to travel 6 stops up the road! At the 2nd shop I entered, I decided to vent
my angst at the FACT that it was the first time I had caught public transport for ages
"In actual fact, I haven't been in a vehicle since the beginning of March," she rages.
Anyway. Bottom line is, it was good to get out to do something NORMAL? for a change .
Now I'm going to have to look at my life from a different perspective, so I can rearrange
things to fit in with the current restraints. Back to the drawing board Blod bach.
Perhaps you need to consider accepting and taking on your role, as a modern day MATRIARCH!

(bach - Welsh for little/small)

WAKE UP

I've been wanting to write this for quite some time now,
but I have been worried that it might cause a row.
What has become of us as a nation,
that makes us fearful of retaliation?
Before LOCKDOWN the streets had a particular type of trash,
but while those food chains were closed, the streets were awash
with surgical face masks and blue vinyl gloves!
What's to become of our environment that nobody loves
enough to keep clean and tidy. Are their homes the same
I ask myself? What is going on? Who's to blame?
Then there are people who spit on the pavement! (Do they do that in their abode?)
Why can't they take a few steps more and gob in the road
I have a friend who lives in a beautiful Welsh town,
where the local folk are now wearing a frown.
Tourists have descended there in their droves,
leaving rubbish everywhere. It behoves
us all to clear up the mess we make,
and not leave it to others for goodness sake!
I have another friend who lives in Penzance,
where the visitors really do take a chance.
They are literally shitting on the beach!
I get that the loo's are closed, and I don't want to preach,
but why can't they bag it up and take it home,
along with the rest of their trash? I'm having a moan,
I know! But we've become such a throwaway
society, that it's hard to see where it will end one day.
Bottom line is. We need to get our act together,
and be the GUARDIANS we're intended to be. Whatever
your persuasion, colour, creed or Spiritual calling,

when Mother Earth fights back, don't start bawling.
We'll have brought it all upon ourselves. Will you wait
for me to be proved right, or WAKE UP before it's too late?

MY MUSINGS!

I care about the environment, so I take my litter home if I can't find a bin.
I often wonder what some people's homes are like, what mess do they live in?
A lot of litter lying around, is harmful in so many ways. Wildlife can't always survive it,
and are trapped 'til the end of their days! When did you last consider, even a little bit,
the impact you're having on our planet, in oh so many ways?
Have you stopped to consider what we're doing, does it matter for future days?
I'm not saying I'm perfect. That's very far from the truth,
but I've become more aware in my dotage, than I was in my misspent youth!
I try to cut down on the water I use, as it is our most precious resource.
There's an old poem about flushing the toilet, that I didn't write of course!
Bottom line is, you don't need to flush after every piddle,
I feel it's obvious when you need to flush, it truly 'ain't a riddle!
We all need to wake up and smell the coffee, which we need water to make.
We also need water to grow it etc etc, for goodness sake!
So next time you put on the kettle, have you filled it with more than you need?
I hope that my musings have at least planted a seed.

CLIFF HANGER?

I'm sitting here feeling very dejected, as I've a sense of what's going on.
I feel we're being brought to the edge of extinction, like many species now gone.
Each day it seems that the goal posts are being moved close to the edge of a cliff,
so before we know it, we'll be like the lemmings if you get my drift.

I truly want to be more positive, and help others to lift their mood,
but I'm finding it really difficult to not just sit here and brood!
I have lots of things to get on with. I need to start my day.
Give up and give in to their unrealistic orders? Not if I can help it. No way.
I feel that the impact of what's being done to us, will continue for many more years.
The thought of what will become of the children now, and those to come, is ONE OF my fears.

XMAS 2020

'Tis the season to be jolly,
just don't look for any holly
as non-essential journeys aren't allowed!
What size turkey will you order, as you cannot feed a crowd?
Will a delivery slot be available for you to get your Xmas cheer?
Or will you need to venture to your local shop that isn't all that near?
Can you really face the long queues to post your cards and gifts?
Perhaps you might say "sod it all", causing major rifts
amongst your family and friends. Who knows how it will pan out
at this festive time of year? You'll sort it - no doubt.

CHAPTER 3

MENTAL HEALTH CHALLENGES

PEER SUPPORT

Those of us who've experienced a journey in Mental Health
Feel that PEER SUPPORT availability would have saved a lot of NHS wealth.
We believe that if it had been offered as soon as we needed it,
the time we spent recovering would definitely have been split -
or at least reduced by a significant amount.
Are our needs REALLY taken into account?
There should be a standard where one is trained to offer support to people who are in need -
of someone who really understands, having been there. Indeed -
it goes without saying that it's cost,
and gives us the chance to be reflective
about where we've come from and are going to.
We can look at the whole experience from a different view.
So please take PEER SUPPORT seriously,
and wisely invest your time and your money.

CAMHS

"IT'S NOT OK TO FEEL BLUE and other lies"
is a book that definitely defies
the stigma around mental health.
I have just started to read the wealth
of many experiences. They're in the public eye
and the book is aimed at the youth of today.
I know! I'm no spring chicken, but hey,
give me a break, every dog has its day.
Anyway. I still feel 16 inside,
so please let me have some pride.
Bottom line is my message to you
is there is some support - it's true.
There's a charity called SHOUT
and the book is about
raising money for the cause.
So pass on the info without pause
to help our young people cope.
WE REALLY NEED TO GIVE THEM HOPE.

IMAGINE!

I'm not really unhappy, just being a miserable so and so.
I don't think it helped being woken up 2.30am for food -
by Mr Tibbs - who's been sent to try my patience and put me in a bad mood!
Every bloody day though - it really is beyond a joke.
I've had him for 8 years now, and he didn't last with previous folk!
I don't need to try and imagine why (although not told) he was a rescue cat.
He's been hard work, to say the least, there's no doubt of that.

Anyway. Now I'm listening to some music that helped to cheer me.
Going back to the first line. Thinking that at the time, made me laugh and helped me to see,
that all is not lost, if you can laugh at yourself,
and I really do know, that laughter's good for my mental health.

I DON'T RECALL ANY!

My get up and go has got up and gone!
Where has it disappeared to? What went wrong?
Is it an age thing, or have I just lost interest?
What's really happening to cause this unrest?
So many questions roaming around my head.
Never really knowing WHY I get out of bed!
Where am I heading with the things that I do?
I can't get answers from me, never mind you!
I'm talking to myself most of the time.
To have someone to share with would be sublime.
I keep on hoping for more than I'm getting
and I'm finding aspects of life quite upsetting.
Onwards and upwards is what I've been saying,
for things to improve I've kept on praying.
My mental health goes up and down,
but overall it is of no renown.
At least I haven't been sectioned for the last 20 years,
I have to be honest, it's one of my greatest fears!
I really don't want to go back there again,
a place to RECOVER, as and when?
The last time they kept me for much longer than was needed,
their disbelief of my truth superseded
the fact that I was back to myself TOTALLY.

They just wouldn't listen to me,
when I told them it was the mind games my one-time friend had played. Names?
I don't recall any. Just as well I think,
'cos I don't want to go back and cause a stink.
Hopefully they are all long gone and on a different path.
You know I was drug tested for having a laugh.
A guy and I were in the smoking room making jokes when
a member of staff walked in and then
said "What are you laughing at?" in a voice full of anger and disbelief.
We were trying to cheer up the others and bring some relief
to the boredom of being there day in and out
with nothing to do. I have no doubt
it was her who arranged to have us tested.
She was the sort of woman who wouldn't have rested,
until she'd found her answer to us having some fun
in a situation where she felt we should be totally glum.
I am glad to say that things are improving
as some of us are getting things moving
where mental health services are concerned.
We are pushing for what we once yearned
for, to be put in place,
there are a number of us - our saving grace.
We work hard to improve what's available
to enable others to become more stable.
We don't just aim to help our peers,
but work with others to reduce their fears
of us and others who have lost their way.
We do all that we can at the end of the day.
So take heart from the fact that we can
make a difference in life. Rather than
sitting wondering and worrying, get off your arse
and see what's available and not a farce.

COMMUNING WITH THE ANCESTORS

One minute I was sitting on the futon I once had,
the next I was being dragged through the doorway
with hands cuffed behind my back and that was very bad!
The sarong I had around me was nowhere in sight - no way
to keep my dignity
let alone my sanity.

I kept my eyes tight shut as they threw me on the trolley waiting there.
I can't recall which of the three types of cuffs were used on me that time,
but believe me - the way I was treated was extremely unfair.
I laughed and joked with whoever they were - eyes still closed - I'd committed no crime.
I was naked as a new-born child,
but their treatment of me had been far from mild!

I was communing with the Ancestors - all the way down the line.
I'm referring to the Spiritual teachers who had joined me to share their knowledge.
They had a lot to teach me, their wisdom knew no bounds. I was doing fine -
but someone had seen it differently and thought I'd gone over the edge
into a place apart from reality.
They obviously misunderstood Spirituality!

To this day, I don't have a clue who that was!
I do recall coming to eventually in a hospital bed with a blanket I'd made -
as someone had covered me with it when they got me outside because
as I told you before I was starkers! I have to be honest I was really afraid
of having to face people again
when I was let out of hospital - as and when!
Now I'm many years down the line
and getting on with life. I guess I'm fine.

PALINDROME

All my life I've buried the grief over the loss of many things.
Never being allowed to express it in a way that brings -
relief and surcease, to an aching and broken heart.
There's a lot to deal with, but where to start?
If I open the floodgates holding back my tears,
will I be crying for as many years -
as I spent pushing them down, deep inside -
holding my head up with a false sense of pride?

There were the odd times I just couldn't hold them back
and I know they were perceived as a lack
on my part. Nasty, negative comments were made
to the point where I was far too afraid
to let the tears of sorrow flow.
So I continued to bury all the many hurts and pains and not let them show.
Now I'm sitting here grieving over yet another loss -
of a so-called friend, who didn't really give a toss.
Ok! I'm the one who's finally had enough and said "no more
of the way you're taking the piss", but felt sad as they walked out the door.

That makes two people this year now who I've sent on their way
and it's only the the second month and the second day!
I've decided no more toxic relationships for me.
I'd rather be on my own than put up with all the misery
of being treated as a convenience when it suits THEIR needs.
I'm giving myself the freedom to move on and sow new seeds.
I know! In some ways I've already been doing just that
and the whole scenario's become old hat.

Written on the 02/02/2020 a PALINDROME.
Last one was 909 years ago on the 11/11/1111.
Next is in 101 years on the 12/12/2121.
After that it will be on the 03/03/3030.

THE SPARK INSIDE

More years ago than I can remember, I fell into a deep dark pit.
There was no-one around to help me out, I just had to get on with it.
I blindly felt my way around the walls and I had to take it really slow,
I hoped and prayed that somehow, a way out would show.
I finally found an opening that was big enough to walk through,
so I gingerly stepped inside, but there was nothing there to view.
You see, all around me was pitch black and not a glimmer of light -
as I edged carefully forward I was given a terrible fright!
The tunnel was collapsing behind me as I made my way,
so there was no going back in the hope of rescue at the end of the day.
Somewhere deep inside me, I knew that the tunnel must end -
but keeping faith it would happen, almost sent me 'round the bend.
Day in and out it went on and on for a multitude of years,
and I felt that if there was no light at the end of the tunnel, I'd be reduced to tears.
I'd already cried an ocean that I didn't know how to reduce,
all I could put it down to was all the years of abuse.
There's a reason for sharing my deep and dark depths of despair,
as I want you and others to know, I too have been there.
So have other people who may not be able to talk about how they feel.
But please, believe me when I say, that where I've been is real.
I found a tiny speck of light that I nurtured and helped to grow.
I'm not saying it happened overnight, the process was very slow.
I won't tell you it's been easy, that would be a blatant lie.
Just don't give up on yourself, keep moving forward, you owe it to the spark inside to give it a try.

25th MAY BANK HOLIDAY

Stressful situations abound in life.
Problem is, they cause me a HELL of a lot of strife!
I was up at silly o'clock again today,
and I had challenges to deal with before I got underway.
It's now past lunchtime and I've just eaten!
I've done the best I can to try and not be beaten -
by trying to deal with what I've had to face.
My head's been all over the bloody place.
Not just that, I've been churning unbelievably inside,
and there's absolutely nowhere I can go and hide -
from the feelings that have been stirred and raised.
It struck me while this was going on, that I was never praised
for anything I ever did. The realisation hit me like a bolt of lightning!
Feeling incapable and inadequate is VERY frightening.

MY ENDEAVOUR

I'm feeling really sad, because I have come to my senses in some way!
There are some very toxic people in my life, and that was difficult to say!
There have been many times in my journey through life,
when I have attracted individuals, who love to create strife!
What exactly does this say about me?
Is it a case of I have too much empathy?
I endeavour to see the best in those that I meet,
but sometimes it just doesn't work out leaving me beat.
Then I have to walk away from the situation that's caused me stress,
but it takes me a long time to accept and acknowledge the mess!
That's because I've kept on attempting to reach their decent side,

something they showed at first, before they took me for a ride!
Where exactly am I going with this narrative? I don't really know!
I just hope that I will continue to learn and grow.

THINKING AGAIN!!!

I'm not having any therapy these days,
so I have to deal with stress in other ways.
I spend an inordinate amount of time talking to myself!
It's one of the ways I try to use to hang on to my mental health.

But I have started to worry at times walking down the road -
when the odd word pops out 'cos my head's in overload!
I really do think far too much and find it hard to switch off.
This over thinking is a bloody nightmare and really tough.
To be honest, my pussy has started to play a big part.

Stroking, caressing and having a scratch right from the start -
works really well to slow my thought processes down.
I'll be concentrating on the pleasure I get from his fur
and feeling the vibrations of his almost silent purr.

I'll be lost in the moment, not focused on anything,
not worrying about all that needs to be done and what the day may bring.
Then all of a sudden I'm brought back to the here and now -
where the little sod's just bitten me, bringing a crease to my brow.

"What the fuck was that for you rotten little git?
Go on, get off my lap now and let me get on with it."
I get up and head for the kitchen to make a brew -
bring it back, sit down and start thinking again, it's true!

THE END

I'm sitting here crying
'cos I knew you were lying
to me. So many times it happened, I chose to ignore
my instincts. Do I really need to say more?
You used and abused me, then tossed me away -
leaving me feeling like shit at the end of the day.
You kept making promises you never did keep
and I'd toss and turn at night, trying to get some much needed sleep.
You'd come back into my life again when it suited your needs -
forgetting the way you'd been treating me as you carried out your deeds.
You will never know how deep the pain you've caused me has gone.
The fact is, I allowed it to happen when the day is done.
But you took advantage of how you knew I felt
and just how to manipulate me so you'd get my heart to melt.
Again and again you've come back to me,
now I've really come to the end you see.
I've made the decision to salvage my pride
and own up to the feelings buried deep inside.
Pain, hurt, anger and so much loss.
Frustration at knowing you never gave a toss -
about me as a woman who cared for you truly.
You acted like a child who is extremely unruly.
You rode roughshod over my every feeling,
leaving me bedazzled, bewildered and with my head reeling.
How I kept my sanity, I will never know!
I AM moving on now so that I can continue to grow.

CHAPTER 4

A PLETHORA OF POEMS

2 BIRDS

My sense of humour has gone walkabout!
I miss its presence, there is no doubt.
I need it more than ever in the current times,
not just for me, but to create my rhymes.
I know it helps to lift peoples moods,
and bring about new attitudes.
I was told way back in the '90's, when talking
to a man called John, (he thought I was baulking)
not to lose my sense of humour, as I would need it in the future!
The time is here and now.

CRADLE TO THE GRAVE

I've always had a fascination with certain tales,
maybe that's because I hail from Wales!
Have you heard the story of Gelert the hound,
whose unfair demise, was extremely profound?

Prince Llewelyn the Great, left him babysitting,
whilst he went off to do some hunting!
An unexpected visitor came calling,
which could have left the prince bawling.
If it hadn't been for Gelert, that would have been the case.
He rose to the occasion, ending up with blood on his face!

The prince returned and taking it all in with a glance,
made his decision and took a stance.
He drew his sword from its sheath
and he slew his hound. Then from beneath
the upturned cradle, came the welcome sound of his child's cry!
Poor Gelert hadn't deserved to die.
Behind the cradle lay the corpse of the wolf Gelert had slain,
and that is how Beddgelert got its name!

The story made me cry, when I heard it in my school,
that's NOT supposed to happen, is the unwritten rule.
I guess I was seen as a soft touch, in many more ways than one,
but I felt the injustice of what to poor faithful Gelert was done.
I believe that the message we've been given here,
is don't rush in, be very careful and clear
about how to act in the here and now.
You can try to think of the consequences and don't allow
yourself to be triggered by frustration, anger, fear or rage.
Do you get where I am coming from? Are we on the same page?

OUR SPARK

A solar flare hit the earth in 1859.
Sparks flew from the equipment for the telegraph line -
giving electric shocks and even starting fires!

Can you imagine the thinking this inspires -
in me? We need to wake up and face reality -
and find once again OUR SPARK of humanity.
Something's not right about the way we're currently living -
where it's mostly take and very little giving.
Where it's each for themself and no sense of community.
We need to/must work toward creating a unity -
of SPIRIT, 'cos the way things are trending
every one of us will be spending
a LOT of the time on our hands
in an even more messed up world, that no-one understands.

UNCANNY?

I'm sitting, here trying to work out how my life got in such a bloody mess!
Oh! I know. It was all the many years of absolute and total distress.
I'm not bitter and twisted about all the shit life's put me through.
Instead, I have tried to turn it into compost and grow good things - it's true.
The truth of the matter is, now it all boils down to struggling with my health.
Trying to be taken seriously about the situations, was stressful in and of itself!
I lost friends along the way, as I guess they just saw me as a moody and miserable bitch.
Someone who did nothing but moan and complain. Coming from some, that was really rich!
They were never around to offer the help and support I so desperately needed.
Even the guy living with me at the time, couldn't see, no matter how I pleaded
for his help to get the most simple of things done. He always had his reasonable? excuses.
I have to be honest, for all the years we lived together, in his eyes, I guess I had my uses.
Of course, I don't know if he would admit to that, even now. But I have come to realise,
it was all part and parcel of MY journey in life. It took me down new paths - a huge surprise,
'cos when he moved out in '97, I had no idea how I'd ever manage to cope on my own.
You see, from the day I was born in '53, I'd always lived with others, and now I was alone!

In an odd sort of way, I have gone from strength to strength, and I can now look back
to see that I was always THERE for other people. But as for my 'SELF', there was a complete lack,
a lack of compassion, love and caring, and I didn't have a clue how to take care of ME!
Who the heck was I anyway? I'd ALWAYS tried to do my best in reality!
For the last 4 months I have been processing like mad! It's been going on for ages anyway,
but now, during the current pandemic, I have little else to do from day to day.
Living with just my problematic cat for company, means I really miss the life I had finally created.
A good thing too, as my old way of life was completely outdated!
It really started coming together around this time last year. I met an amazing woman in a caf
called Heaven.
(We hit it off straight away, and swapped phone numbers before she went on her way.)
The synchronicity has been happening off and on since, and I've chosen an unexpected profession!
Thanks to meeting Jenessa, I pulled some of my poems together and wrote a lot more.
Then my friend Marie typed them up, in a format that helped to open the door.
As I'm a technophobe, and can only do so much, Jan forwarded the manuscript to Danni.
The way the whole thing came together, was ever so uncanny!
I already had the cover image for my book, of a wolf howling at the moon,
my sister Ro had sent me it years before, it wasn't a moment too soon!
As for the caricature that went with the bio, that was done by Morris at Jos' Azawala cafe.
You know I have come to realise - it's true, every dog has it's day!

THE LINK

I plucked my whiskers and put on a bra,
I wasn't intending on going far!
I was about to sit on the chair I call "The Throne" -
to be interviewed online, in my own home!

My book of poems "MOONSTRUCK" was now on sale,
and some of the content is beyond the pale!
I was ready and waiting for the appointed time,
trying to decide if I should be sublime.

I got the link and was soon connected -
must have been the right choice I selected!
After all the effort and setbacks we'd gone through,
for reasons I can't go into, we had to cancel, it's true!

HOLM OAK

I stand here, surveying all who pass me by.
I can't recall when I started, and I'm not even going to try.
I have stood sentinel as I have grown,
from the acorn that was planted, after I was brought from home.
The memory that is deep in me, is of warm and sunny climes,
of falling from my mother tree in far off distant times.
My canopy's a constant shelter, for things that live on me,
but when two leggéds look my way, they only see a tree!
Sometimes they get really close, and I feel THEIR SAP rising!
I honestly didn't think they had it in them! It's always really surprising.
Occasionally, some four leggéds, do their best to water me,
and I just have to stand and take it, after all I'm just a tree!
Or is that your assumption of the role I'm here to play?
What do think you are breathing in, each and every day?
I have many uses, of which you're not aware,
I don't just stand here looking pretty, I produce your very air!
Without myself and all my relations, you couldn't even exist.
So think on this when you see me next, would my absence even be noticed?

FROM THE HEART

There have been very rare occasions in my life, when I have been overwhelmed
by a truly amazing feeling.
It is so powerful, all encompassing, beautiful, yet short lived and leaves me reeling -
from the onslaught and suddenness of its appearance.
There truly aren't the words in my language to give it credence!
I wish there was a way to share it with all of humanity,
and it might help to put an end to the insanity -
of what is being done in the name of GREED.
When you look at what NATURE freely provides us, is there really a need -
to keep taking and taking without giving back?
It's not even as if there's a total lack.
I am as guilty as the next one of forgetting my good intentions,
but this is something nobody ever really mentions.
How can I find a way to impart,
what I'm saying, comes from the heart?

SHOW

Stop your Stressing.
Stop your Hurrying.
Stop your Obsessing.
Stop your Worrying.

Take time out just to be.
Look around and set yourself free.
Notice the colours of the day.

Let Mother Nature have her way.
Inhale her scents after the rain -
it will help to wash away your pain.
Look at the plants now, so clear and bright -
with raindrops glistening in the suns light.

MATERNAL HAPLOGROUP YAMNAYA

It's taken many years and a lot of mostly difficult lessons to grow into me!
"Where the heck is she coming from? What the dickens is she meant to be?"
I now look at life in a MUCH different way.
We are all skeletons under our skin at the end of the day.
As far as I'm aware, we all bleed red blood don't we?
I know! The space suit we walk around in makes it easy to see -
we're originally from different areas of this planet we call home.
Some didn't choose where they've ended up, others chose to roam.
I have a percentage of Neanderthal blood
and can be traced way back to Eastern Africa - it's all good.
I can only trace back my maternal line -
7,500 years to the Yamnaya, who were nomadic pastoralists - that's fine.
They were from the Steppes of Eurasia and moved west.
Now I'm mainly of British and Irish descent according to my test.
That would have pissed my mother off no end.
To realise she had a lot of Irish blood, might have sent her 'round the bend.
Bottom line is, she was VERY racist and mostly hid it well.
But when it came to certain groups, there's a different tale to tell.
She fancied Sidney Poitier and I recall her winding up my brother about having a black baby.
She chose to forget all that when I started dating a man from a different race.
Maybe it was one rule for her, and another for her eldest daughter!

FOR NOW!

Be careful what you wear in bed
(that's if you do)
as what I was wearing (a black robe that showed up blue) bled
all over my white brushed cotton sheet!
(We used to call it flannelette - but that 'ain't a trendy sound, is it?)
(Anyway I digress!)
To be honest - wearing nothing is really neat.
But hey! I have to do the unusual at times,
or I wouldn't be able to write my rhymes!
This is my second one today.
I'm wondering where they've come from I have to say.
It's not as if I've ignored my chores,
my bedding's washed - but not my drawers.
(I mean the ones in the kitchen!)
My pussy's been sorted too.
I mean my cat, what's wrong with you?
My bed is half made, I just need to sort the pillows out.
Putting them in their covers does my hands in. Arthritis, not gout.
I need to put my clean clothes away (including my drawers).
Then find some time to have fun and play -
with some fabric and cotton.
The thoughts you're having about this are rotten!
Your mind is a cesspit I have to say.
Now I'm off to finish making my bed
and have a think whether enough's been said (for now).
My bed's now sorted, but not my clothes.
I can do that later I suppose.

I did sort out some fabric for when I'm ready,
but as for time, patience and holding my hands steady -
well, I'll just have to wait and see.
Now I'm going to sort out a cake and a cup of tea.

SHEER BLOODY LUXURY

When I was a lass, we didn't have an inside loo -
we had to go outside to do a wee and a poo!
Our outdoor lav didn't flush. In fact, it was just a bucket!
The seat was a wooden board with a round hole cut in it.
In winter you had to rush there and back -
'cos if you didn't your cheeks might crack!
I won't tell you how good the potatoes etc. tasted -
having been grown in what we'd all defecated!

It was when we lived there I went to school on a steam train,
Beeching's cuts happened after that and things just weren't the same.
It was around that time that calculators came out -
they made life easier - there is no doubt.
But we weren't allowed to use 'em, it was classed as cheating!
They were very big anyway and there's no beating
what's available these days. Mobiles are small and neat -
containing everything you need.
Technological advances have moved on indeed.
But I question if it's for the better at times -
although Google does help me with stuff and some rhymes.

Ok! When we moved up to the village to reside -
we had to use the phone box that no one pissed inside!
We had to use two old pennies to make a call -
moving up the social ladder, my parents had the wherewithal
to have a phone installed. Trouble was, it was a party line -
so if the neighbour's weren't using it, it worked out fine.
(They were always on the bloody phone though!)

I could talk about all the years with no central heating.
The pleasure of having a real fire there is just no beating!
I know it's not PC to burn fossil fuel these days -
but there are elements of the old ways
that we have sadly lost
and at what an enormous cost!
We weren't such a throwaway society.
Things were made to last and not cause us anxiety.
Shoes went to the cobblers to be soled and heeled -
ways to make do and mend, in women's magazines were revealed.
We didn't have convenience food, we had to start from scratch
and the taste of what we had, these days you just can't match!
There was no paying more for organic, as our food already was.
We were told technological advances would help us because -
we would have more leisure time to do what we enjoyed.
They didn't say it would reach a point of being unemployed!
A lot of what's been invented, has taken away our skills -
so we've become surplus to requirements and dealing with our ills.

There's a helluva lot more I could go on and on about -
but I'd bore you to tears I have no doubt.
So instead, I'll get myself together and get on with the day -
where I do the dishes etc. Buy a dishwasher? No way!

NUMB BUM SYNDROME!

I've ordered a doughnut ring cushion, to relieve the pain in my arse.
I've reached a point in my life now, where I'm totally sick of the farce.
I keep rearranging the cushions to try and ease the pain,
but before I can get comfy, I have to do it again!
I slipped on ice many years ago, and damaged my tail bone,
add to that the fact that my bum is mostly not in tone!
There's very little flesh there to help ease the discomfort,
although there's plenty elsewhere I can report.
Anyway, according to a BMI done months ago,
I'm classed as obese these days I'll have you know!
There is still not enough flesh there to help me feel at ease,
I want my cushion to arrive as soon as possible - please.

RABBIT!

There's absolutely no way I can say NO when my pussy really wants something!
I just can't deny it when it persists and insists on having!
It leaves me feeling extremely frustrated -
as I fork out a lot for what seems to be underrated.
He just won't touch rabbit, beef or that kind of cat food.
In fact he'll only eat one selection of one brand - he's shrewd.
He also looks like the cat on the box,
with his part white face, chest and socks.
Anyway, there are foods I eat that he DEMANDS I share,
so it's a good thing that for him I really do care!

A REFLECTION

Some people act as if they're a paragon of virtue,
as if butter wouldn't melt in their mouth - not true.
They hide behind the words they learnt to talk,
but on that path they don't always walk!
We often see a reflection of self in others,
but don't acknowledge it as it bothers -
us to admit to OUR failings.
Instead we continue our railings -
against the person we perceive as fair game to attack.
We often ignore OUR total lack -
of real empathy, care and concern.
We choose to override our intuition and not learn
to be at one with another and hold our SELF in check.
Instead, we end up giving it to them in the neck!

SAY NOTHING

There's something going through my mind about children.
We were all a child once, both women and men.
I feel that many of us have a wounded child deep inside,
but we were never given the tools to help us ride
through the challenges LIFE throws our way.
We're raised to, SAY NOTHING to anyone, at the end of the day.
The problem is (as I see it) we're perpetuating abuse through ignorance.
We wander through life, and very often, don't have the chance
to deal with the problems created in our past.
For just how many more generations will this last?
Somehow, we need to find our way forward, as members of the human race.

We must start working on not worrying about saving face.
Let's be real about who we are, when we feel ready to do so.
Of course it would have to be at appropriate times, to help others to grow.
I hope this isn't sounding preachy, but I am sharing from my heart.
Too often we are stuck in our head, thinking that's where to start,
but I have come to realise that not all is as it seems.
Somehow, we need to realise them, and then follow our dreams.

ON ESCAPING FROM A BULLY!

"I am having a celebration, as a result of liberation from domination!"
Said I, with a vodka and lemonade in hand. It was my salutation
to the fact that I had decided to walk away from the things I LOVED doing.
It was the only solution I could come up with, to maintain my sanity, and avoid rueing
giving in to the way I truly wanted to react. I wanted to scream, swear and shout,
rant and rave,
but in professional situations, that just isn't the way you should behave.
The worst thing about it is, that when it first started over a year ago,
I spoke to the individual who was well aware of what they were up to you know!
Anyway. I'm sitting here now writing it down, and the reason for that is this -
there may come a time in your life too, when you have to walk away from people
taking the piss!

C U NEXT TUESDAY!

I've wanted to write about this for a long time,
but I just couldn't think how to create the rhyme.
Anyway, now I am wide awake
and trying to keep occupied for goodness sake!

It's a word that's been given negative undertones,
and at one time I hated it, I'll make no bones.
I once refused to talk to a guy for a week
when he used that word - oh so sleek.
Now I want to reclaim it as a positive,
'cos without it, we wouldn't live.
It's where we all came from, to be here on Earth,
it has definitely been changed to lessen its worth.
I want to ensure that you use it advisedly,
as it has other meanings you see.
Kunti is a Hindu nature goddess!
Has her name been used to cause distress?
Has that too been twisted into the negative - cunt -
so that women bear the brunt
of so many men's misogyny?
I really don't know. You tell me.

WOULD I?

My space suit is getting old and worn, it's not functioning as it should.
It's leaking noxious gases, which really 'ain't no good.
It's been through the wringer many times, and is covered in dark patches.
I really do need to try to sort it out, and batten down the hatches.
I lost my connection to ground control, many years ago!
As for my communication system, well, the batteries are getting low.
My breathing apparatus isn't working as it should,
and the chances of getting anything fixed, well, would I, if I could?

ABSURD FACT?

There's two taboo words that start with 'C',
I have both now, so I guess that gives me
the right to raise the fact .
Just don't expect me to use any tact.
Actually, I will tell it as I see it.
'CUNT' is a word that can land you in shit,
it's one that shocked me when I first heard it used.
Sadly it's something that has been badly abused
in oh so many ways! It was our portal into the world we know.
Like it or not, we are basically here to learn and grow.
I know! For many, the lessons through the years
just aren't easy, we have to face and conquer our fears.
Which brings me to the other taboo word
that we avoid mentioning! Now that's really absurd.
I was told I have bowel cancer, just last week!
Oh my goodness! I've said it now. Was that sleek,
or was I being totally insensitive to your sensibilities?
Or did my bluntness give you the willies?

BETRAYAL

I really trusted you, and believed you were a good friend,
but your recent treatment of me, could have sent me 'round the bend.
This isn't the first time I've been shat on from a great height,
leaving me in a truly desperate plight.
I can think of at least 2 other occasions when it's occurred,

and looking back now, I realise why the edges became blurred.
The reality appears to be, that you claim what was mine as yours,
so you can head off into the sunset to major applause.
Now listen up, and listen well my one time mate,
you just never know what will be your ultimate fate.

LIVE FROM THE HEART

I have always found life difficult to cope with, but somehow I have managed to muddle along!
I don't want to be an adult, all grown up, as I was never allowed to be a child!
When I landed here on Earth from between my mother's legs, I realised I'd got it all wrong.
There was something about the atmosphere that just didn't ring true, and my innocence was soon defiled.

It's time to stop making excuses for what other people do TO us.
That hook we keep letting them off becomes buried deep inside.
(Where on Earth is she heading now? Will she ever stop causing a fuss?)

I have come to believe that we are here on Earth to experience, then spread love, light and joy.
Something has gone drastically wrong through the years, creating untold pain, trauma and abuse
to so many of us humans as well as the rest of creation. We came here to learn, and enjoy
what this beautiful planet offers us freely. But there are the few who have made misuse
of us in oh so many ways! From the cradle to the grave we are conditioned and controlled,
while living with the illusion of freedom. When will the enormity of all that is wrong become clear
to the general populace? When will the virtues of respect, caring, sharing and helping
become the norm, so we can live from the heart, in love and never in fear.

T.O.B

I can almost see my fanny, for the first time in many years,
and my tits have shrunk, almost bringing me to tears.
I loved the way my cleavage once sat there proud and soft,
although I had to wear a bra to keep the buggers aloft!
Now they've reduced to about half the size they were,
and as for something to hold them up, I have to defer.
They always were uncomfortable, but now it's got much worse.
You can tell they were invented by a guy, and became a woman's curse!
Now I'm glad it's winter, and I can get away without wearing one,
but you know the cost of buying a decent bra, really is a con.
Anyway. Now I have joined the T.O.B brigade until at least the spring,
when I'll have to fork out a lot of dosh to stop them hanging!

THE BEAST IS DEAD

I know it's all the pain, grief, frustration and anger, that created the tumour in my bowel.
All the pent up emotions I tried to express were thrown back in my face, so I threw in the towel.
I swallowed all the shit that was heaped upon my head,
always believing I was to blame and I'd be better off dead!
It all stems back to my mother's breast, where her milk was meanly given.
She often told me I was unlovable, and that's where I was riven.
All my life I've believed her words buried deep down inside.
Now I can hold up my head and say something that can't be denied.
I am loved by so many people who have seen what she never did.
It's taken me too many years to reveal what was so sadly hid.
I am a SPIRITUAL HEALER, who had to heal herself first,
but in order do so I had to go through the worst.
My life's been tough to say the very least.

61

Tonight, sitting in a hospital bed, I've slayed the beast.
The reason I'm sharing this with you?
Is to open your eyes to what is true.

Written in the early hours of Sunday 7th February 2021.

LIFE'S JOURNEY

I forgive you mum. I realise now you didn't know any better.
I suppose you could say that this is a kind of letter.
Just to let you know that I'm doing alright in a funny sort of way,
that life's journey has led me here today.
I'm sitting in a hospital bed after having an op.
The last thing I ever expected I would have to cop.
They removed a cancerous tumour from the top right of my bowel.
Some of what I've been through has really made me howl.
But hey, I'm here to tell the tale and move on with my life
I know I've now reached a point to let go of all my strife.

Written in the early hours of Sunday 7th February 2021.

I AM BLESSED

I took my health for granted for many, many years,
and recently discovered one of most people's biggest fears.
After more tests than I want to remember,
I was finally informed last December
that I have bowel cancer! It truly wasn't a shock
as I had a feeling my world might rock

with the news I might be given.
But I took it in my stride,
and yes, even I was very surprised
by my calm acceptance of the news.
There was no point in trying to refuse
the fact as it was presented to me.

I now know that I am truly blessed
to live in a place where we have the NHS.
The doctors, nurses and other staff along the way
were absolutely amazing, and they deserve much better pay.
They work tirelessly, to provide a service that's free
to so many people in this country.
I discovered that I needed them in many ways,
and I will be extremely grateful 'til the end of my days.

CHAPTER 5

Suggestive
Explicit
X-rated

HEDONISM (The pursuit of pleasure; sensual self indulgence.)

Have you ever found yourself in a situation with someone
who is so into THEIR pleasure, that nothing can be done
to shift THEIR need for sexual satisfaction thinking?
I guess it doesn't help when they've been drinking!
Nothing you say or do to get YOUR point across,
makes an iota of difference, THEY just don't give a toss.
YOU'RE considered to be moody, when you're REALLY unwell,
and they don't want to take 'NO' for an answer, truth to tell!
I found myself actually feeling worse after THEIR predatory onslaught!
There are some lessons in life that just can't be taught.

WOW!

You put a spring in my step and an itch in my fanny,
the effect you had on me was really uncanny!
The smile on my face was so hard to erase when you were close by.

But guess where I'm at right now? Exactly 8 months have passed,
and I have seen just how fickle you are at long last.
Truth to tell you managed to pull the wool over my eyes.

Time and time again, you said you aren't like other men,
but that was a blatant lie. In fact you were worse and then
some. I've decided to move on now! Is that a surprise?

SAVAGE

The right sort of music really hits the spot.
It makes me want to go with the rhythm and play - a lot!
Years ago on a hot summer's night -
winding my one time guy up - to his delight?
We were on the dance floor -
I'd had a few drinks and I'd loosened up - need I say more?
Well let me put it this way - I must have turned him on -
'cos by the time we left the party, all my inhibitions had gone!
How we got home, I just don't recall,
but I know he was expecting to have a ball.
I vaguely remember walking in to the flat,
then crashing out on the sofa and no more after that!
These days, moving around is difficult to say the least.
I'm in the days of famine and I miss the feast.

I was listening to "Heaven", a track from the album "Savage" -
Songs like that, time just doesn't seem to ravage -
for me at any rate. Just as well really -
as I enjoy listening to it - clearly!

NAIN (North Wales Welsh for grandmother)

Looking back on where it got to with us,
I'm wondering why I used to make a fuss -
when you finally returned to turn on the charm?
Then I'd give in to you chancing your arm -
it wasn't so much that I couldn't believe my luck,
but (if I'm honest) a case of enjoying a good fuck!
If nain was still alive, she'd (be well old) know just where I'm coming from,
and she'd have REALLY appreciated having HER very own TOM! (Google it. The urban
dictionary, number 4.)
She comes to mind more often these days,
as I can relate even better now, to her eccentric ways.
Now when I'm feeling sad and down, her words pop into my head.
"No use crying over spilt milk, especially if it was because of a table-ender!
It's much more fun than going to bed."

THE BLACK MUG

I just went on a train of thought that led me all over the place!
It started off when I looked at a mug I bought, and the look on my friends face.
It was sitting on the shelf in a charity shop, waiting for me to buy it!
Nain would have loved the sentiment too, and it would have been a hit.
In fact, if she was still alive, I would have considered passing it on.

But sad to say, it's been many years since she left us here - she's long gone.

My memories of her, feed my naughty sense of humour, to say the least.

I often find her words popping into my head and raising the sexual beast.

She made no bones about her love of sex, to me at any rate.

If it wasn't for her, goodness knows what would have been my fate.

Anyway. I digress. The whole point of what I'm saying is, that she liberated me in a funny sort of way. She talked about **SEX** when I'd had my kids, helping set MY THINKING free.

It wasn't really specific, just the occasional tale of something she had done.

She was a real character in my book of amazing women I've known, bar none.

There were also the times she would reveal something intended to shock.

Polaroid pictures of her gay friend's appendage, and an **enormous, heavy, black rubber cock!**

I have to confess that reaching this point in my writing, has brought on gales of laughter.

I'm thinking of whoever gets to here, never seeing me in quite the same way after.

Now I'm thinking of my mother's reaction, after helping Frank clear out nains place.

I'd found the Polaroid pictures, hidden away in various books. But of the cock - not a trace!

It was time for me to head back to my home in London, and I was wondering how to verbalize what I REALLY MUST tell my mother about the missing cock. I didn't want it to be a total surprise

when she came across it, as she inevitably would. Frank must have packed it away in its bag.

Her reaction was as to be expected I suppose, and I'm just now realizing, she considered nain a slag.

Her exact words were - "Oh! The filthy bitch!" A case of pot calling kettle, as she had satisfied her lust.

She'd been married to dad for over 25 years, when it came to light about her and Frank. Unjust is the word that comes to my mind, and that's putting it mildly, as Frank was married too.

My mother acted as though beyond reproach, and would never have gone there. It's true!

I believe that her biggest problem was being born out of wedlock. Not such an issue these days.

When my mother arrived here though, it was "**CONSIDERED A SIN!**" Who coined **THAT** phrase?

Nain had to carry on working to contribute for mums keep with her grandfather and his wife.

I wonder if that was another aspect of her resentment for nain, causing a lot of endless strife?
All I recall growing up, about the odd occasions nain came to stay, apart from her love for me,
was the dreadful way my mother treated her. Granted, nain was a difficult character. That was
plain to see.
Where I'm at now on my walk through life, I take great pride in what she shared.
The truth is, that as a woman she admitted she **LOVED SEX**, and what's more she actually dared
to be up front about her sexploits to a certain extent. She also expressed it in a humorous way.
After doing the IMPROV course last year, I have to admit I sometimes do too, I must say.
Back to where I started off my long-winded, rambling diatribe, and my friends look of shock
when I picked up the black mug, with white writing and a red heart. It says I LOVE COCK.

CONDITIONED FROM BIRTH

Nothing was ever really talked about indoors as I grew up!
SEX education for me was 'Keep your hand on your ha'penny.'
I was told to talk to my bro, and tell him what I knew. But the young pup
already knew the little I had gleaned. He'd been waiting to see if I had any
further information to pass on. Sadly, he's been long gone to the Happy Hunting Grounds.
Now I've come to the realisation, that I know very little about the facts of life,
if you know what I mean? That really isn't as crazy as it probably sounds.
When you think of what I talk about, and how I try to put an end to a lot of strife,
you might possibly consider that I am worldly wise and that I'm a know it all.
Truth to tell, I still have a heck of a lot of learning to do, and I'm enjoying finding out some things
that are a real surprise. The current situation has been an eye opener for me. I've also had time to recall
things that I'd forgotten, or buried deep inside as a way to cope with the emotion it brings.
A lot of it's connected to being conditioned from birth, as a female eldest child.
I really and truly wouldn't have wanted to be here as a man, but being a woman really 'ain't
easy either you know.

But considering that we are the ones actually giving birth etc, guys have it fairly mild in comparison to what a lot of women go through. But I do want to be able to show my feelings, without being rebuffed by a man I end up in a relationship with.

THE NORM???

You just might consider me a prude,
without hearing me out! I consider that rude.
I'm not like most other women you see,
I've come to my senses and faced reality.
I live in a society dominated by men,
who tend to treat us as property, and then
expect us to open our legs and perform,
'cos that's what porn has brainwashed them to think of, as the norm!
The really sad thing is that they're suffering too,
as they're missing out on a real chance to be happy - it's true.
Problem is, that they just don't treat us right.
They call us a COLD BITCH, FRIGID and UPTIGHT.
They really can't see the damage they're doing,
how it's their attitude, and behaviour that gets us eschewing
the sexual advances we can read like a book.
We are well aware that it's often a case of, they just had a look
at their favourite site on Google or Chrome,
because we were busy cooking for them, when they got home!
We weren't ready to attempt to raise their flag,
which would have meant they called us a SLAG.
Then you're a NYMPHOMANIAC, or you're just a TART,
when they can't get an erection, after you made a start
on trying to be, just what they want you to be.
It's your fault that they can't come up with the goods you see,

'cos they just won't accept responsibility for any of their actions.
They actually get a kick from your reactions!
They have to lay blame at your door,
as you are the one in front of them. Need I say more?

I LOVE SEX......

when I can get it!
There have been times I have to admit
when I've felt like a born again virgin -
something that's really quite disturbin'.
When you consider it's how we all got here,
our attitudes around it are very queer!
We're not supposed to confess our interest
in an aspect of life that's taboo at best.
Add to the mix when you're on some medication,
you lose your libido, can't get an erection -
if you're a bloke that is.
Well, put it this way, it causes a tizz.
As for talking about our concerns,
we avoid doing so in case our face burns
with embarrassment for being honest
and in case we cause some unrest.
Instead, we bury our head in the sand
as we don't think people will understand
just where we're coming from. In truth,
they usually believe we're being uncouth.
But that's their problem innit?
Now I'm opening my gob, and we're in it to win it.

ONCE TOO OFTEN!

You've always been economical with the truth -
much to my detriment by strewth.
Just enough honesty to get what you want/desire,
but now it's reached a point that's raised my ire.
You've taken the piss once to often -
and quite conveniently seem to have forgotten
that I PAID you for ALL you did for me.
You came at an exorbitant fee!
I didn't know you would cost sooo much -
I thought it was for gratis as such!
Oh well! I won't go there again,
not with you, how about other men?
I will take my time and get to know their ways -
if that's at all possible these days.

OFF THE HOOK

I've reached the end of my tether where you're concerned.
The lessons have been plentiful, and I have learned
that you remind me of my bloody mother!!!
I really did prefer it, when you acted more like a brother,
rather than a man who gets what HE wants from me.
(I really should know better and consign it to history.)
Then, when I've been conned into subjugation, and a lot more -
you kept clearing off, (having treated me as of no consequence) then you'd return to my door.
More fool me, for falling for your transitory charm.
Truth of the matter is, that I kept ignoring the alarm

that went off each time you disappeared, and finally came back.
I'd be getting on with my life and your reappearance would knock me off track.
It's not even as if you have any feelings for me, is it? I'm just a woman who
was tricked into acknowledging, that I have deep feelings for you!
Well, I've had more than enough, of your nefarious dealings with me.
You hide behind your mask of - 'I'm a decent guy'. I have come to see -
I need to get myself off the hook you caught me on.
It's time for me to recognize that this has been an unbelievable con.
Who benefited the most from the start, to this point in time?
A really truthful answer from you, would be sublime.

NO COMPROMISE

You've let me down - yet again -
having once said, "I'm not like other men."
Well I've got news for you
that is looong overdue -
you aren't any better, in fact you're worse
and falling for you has been a curse.
You managed to hoodwink me from the start,
with your stealth and your lies you captured my heart.
You attempted to change ME into what YOU felt you needed,
you suggested, chivvied, manipulated and proceeded
to build me up to your expectation
of what I should be - no negotiation.
Absolutely no compromise on your part either
and I should accept it all and not mither
you in any way as that would be unacceptable in your eyes.
I'm moving on now. Is that a surprise?

GET AWAY!

There was a time I was having **SEX** with a player!
I ended it and was left with some condoms, lube and my marbles intact!
I have to admit too, my hair was a lot greyer.
He killed the golden goose in fact.
But that's his problem now, as I am getting on with my life.
I'm going in a different direction you see,
I'm getting rid of stress and strife.
But I just want to ask if you can relate with me?
The reason I'm checking it out with you
is because a lot of people do take the piss.
Dig deep in your heart and you will see it's true,
and they don't see anything's amiss!
They go through life treading on everyone's feelings,
using, abusing and blaming them for the issues
that they created with their dishonest dealings.
Get away from them as soon as you can! Save money on tissues!

BROTHERLY LOVE

I am ever hopeful of meeting the right guy -
I've spent enough years having a try!
I mean - the ones I fancy are usually unavailable
and the ones I end up with? Well, they're often unstable,
one way or another.
Or else they're more like a brother!
So. If you happen to know someone who's free -
and looking for love, please, introduce them to me.

I know! It may NOT work out - again.
That seems to be a problem with me and men.
But hey! I'll keep on trying.
To say I won't - well, I'd be lying.

Lightning Source UK Ltd.
Milton Keynes UK
UKHW030112170222
398804UK00003B/8